The Birth of a Widow

The Birth of a Widow

Collected Poems

by

Kathie Giorgio

Cover design by Shay Culligan
Cover image *Orange Thoughts* by Jesse Lee Kercheval
Author photo by Ron Wimmer, Wimmer Photography

ISBN: 979-8-90146-719-0
Library of Congress Control Number: 2026931893

Kelsay Books
502 South 1040 East, A-119
American Fork, Utah 84003
Kelsaybooks.com

This book is dedicated, of course, to Michael Giorgio.
Our relationship continues always.

Acknowledgments

The following poems from this collection have been previously published:

Creative Wisconsin: “The Cliché”

Months To Years: “The Forest”

Contents

Other Books by Kathie Giorgio

Novels

Don't Let Me Keep You (Black Rose Writing, 2024)
Hope Always Rises (Black Rose Writing, 2023)
All Told (Austin Macauley Publishers, 2022)
If You Tame Me (Black Rose Writing, 2019)
In Grace's Time (Black Rose Writing, 2017)
Rise From the River (The Main Street Rag Publishing Company, 2015)
Learning to Tell (A Life)Time (The Main Street Rag Publishing Company, 2013)
The Home for Wayward Clocks (The Main Street Rag Publishing Company, 2011)

Prose Collections

Today's Moment of Happiness Despite the News: A Year of Spontaneous Essays (Black Rose Writing, 2018)
Oddities & Endings; The Collected Stories of Kathie Giorgio (The Main Street Rag Publishing Company, 2016)
Enlarged Hearts: Stories (The Main Street Rag Publishing Company, 2012)

Poetry Collections

Let Me Tell You, Let Me Sing! (Kelsay Books, 2025)
Olivia in Five, Seven, Five: Autism in Haiku (Finishing Line Press, 2022)
No Matter Which Way You Look, There Is More to See (Finishing Line Press, 2020)
When You Finally Said No (Finishing Line Press, 2019)
True Light Falls in Many Forms (The Main Street Rag Publishing Company, 2016)

Author's Note

When I woke up on the morning of January 17, 2024, my mind was only on my schedule and the work that lay ahead. It was a Wednesday, and Wednesdays are one of my busiest days. I own and run an international creative writing studio, AllWriters' Workplace & Workshop LLC. For the last twenty years, I've worked at least 85 hours a week, running the business, and teaching thousands of writers how to survive in this very odd career. On Wednesdays, I have six one-on-one coaching clients and I teach a workshop in the afternoon, so my mind was on my students and the steps necessary to get through my day.

I was on Zoom with my 6:00 p.m. client when I saw my phone light up with an unfamiliar number. I ignored it and let it go to voicemail. In the scant two minutes I had between my 6:00 and 7:00 clients, I called in. A stressed voice told me that my husband was in the ER and that I needed to call back as soon as I could. I hit redial immediately and was told that Michael was struck and run over by a passenger van as he crossed an intersection to get from his job to his bus stop home. The voice on the phone said, "Get here! Hurry!"

Our lives changed right then. My husband, Michael's life actually ended, but he was resuscitated by a witness, a retired Navy rescuer. Michael was in the crosswalk and walking with the light. From witness accounts, the driver was speeding, ran a red light, and plowed right into Michael before running him over with all four tires. Michael suffered multiple skull fractures, a severe traumatic brain injury, brain bleeds, brain swelling, a back fracture, a possible neck fracture, a fracture of the left tibia, two fractured ribs, the loss of hearing in his left ear, and the loss of sight in his left eye.

One of the most ironic things? Michael didn't drive. He was phobic about driving, and his biggest nightmare, literally, was being hit by a vehicle.

The driver was only given a citation for failure to yield to a pedestrian. He paid a $73 fine. He wasn't even tested for drinking or drugs at the scene.

Over the next five months, we went through trauma after trauma. Michael went back and forth between the neurological ICU and step-down rooms for six weeks. Then he was off to rehab for three weeks. He came home with home health care, returned to the hospital, came home again, and then returned to the hospital for the final time. On Friday, June 14th, as Michael's power of attorney, I elected to remove all life support, including nutritional support, and Michael was transported to hospice. On June 19th, early in the morning, our daughter Olivia and I were by his side as Michael released his last breath.

Michael's life ended. Mine changed yet again.

It has now been a year since Michael's death. During that year, I read these two sentences from Ann Patchett's novel, Tom Lake: *I understood what was happening. But I didn't understand it was happening to me.*

I shook with the stark reality of it.

Sixty-six days after Michael's death, I arrived on the Oregon coast in the little town of Waldport. I've been coming here almost every year since 2006 for my own personal writing retreat. When I'm here, I am only me—I leave all of my other roles behind. I'm not a wife, a mother, a teacher, a business owner. I'm just me, and as I identify most profoundly with "writer", that's who I am. I write here. I live the life I've always wanted to live.

But that year, 2024, I showed up here with a new and very unexpected role. Widow.

Before I'd arrived, I'd written one poem about Michael's death. But here, with the ocean in my backyard, I suddenly burst into poetry. All about Michael, about what happened to him, what happened to me, what happened to us. The relief in finding the words was soul-soaking.

So I decided to let the poems come as they chose—I did not sit down on any given day and think, I'm going to write a poem about . . . Instead, as the words and lines and stanzas came, I wrote them.

The poems are dated on the day they were first written, but the events are not in order. I decided I would let this evolve for the first year after Michael died, and at that point, I would stop looking behind me and start looking ahead.

And that's what I've done.

Is my grieving over? Not by a long shot. But is it transitioning into something manageable, something that I can walk beside, rather than being fully underwater? And can I start opening my view again to the rest of my life, who I am, who is around me, and what I want to accomplish?

Yes.

So this is *The Birth of a Widow.*

The Forest

Prose Poem
August 1, 2024

Even after sharing what could be good news, the doctor still clarifies. “Your husband is not out of the woods yet,” he says. “He is in the woods. Deep, deep in the woods. All he can see are the trees.” I look at you then, lying in your hospital bed, sheets like snow, crisp, clean, cold. White blanket. White pillow. Winter. So different than the red that surrounded you when I first came upon you in the ER, red, like the leaves of Autumn. In Winter, you are motionless. You are alone in the forest, and you make no sound. The skin between your eyebrows puckers and so I call your name. Your skin smooths every time.

I worry that you are lost in the woods. I call your name, over and over. But I hope the forest you are in is beautiful. I hope the green is bright. I wish for birdsong. The flight of a sandhill crane, the trill of a sparrow. The flash of a deer. A stream, with impossible golden fish. The sun in the trees, that little bit of good news. A daffodil in the middle of all that green.

I don’t know then that you will at first find your way. My voice guides you, calls you home. I don’t know then that, after reaching for me, you will turn, look over your shoulder, and return to the forest. Go back, even after your memory appears, disappears, reappears like the sun through the trees. After you manage to walk up two flights of stairs to our third-floor deck and you sit in the sun with a smile that not only rivals the sunlight, but makes the sun seem as small as that daffodil. As small as that good news felt, on the day of snow and forest. On the deck, you are surrounded by our flowers. We move into Spring.

Oh, the glow of your smile. Your skin smooth. Your eyes on me.

But you return to the woods and you lose your way. Even though I call your name. Over and over. Until I have no voice left. You look over your shoulder, glow that smile, and then you're gone.

I hope the forest is beautiful. I hope the sun comes back. There is no Summer. Oh, to see your smile.

Return to Oregon

Written on retreat in Waldport, Oregon
August 24, 2024

When I was here a year ago
my husband was still alive.
He hadn't yet been hit by a passenger van
as he walked across a busy street in January
to get to the bus that would bring him
Home.

When I was here a year ago
he texted me several times a day
We talked on the phone.
And at night, we watched *The Waltons*
my favorite TV show
him at home on the television in our
living room
me here in Oregon, the ocean right outside
my door
our phones set to speaker and we discussed
the show. And our days.
Together.
2179.9 miles apart.

When I was here a year ago
every time we spoke
via text, email, or phone
we said *Goodbye.* We said *I love you.*
I didn't know then how soon our goodbyes
our I love yous
would be our last.
How soon we would be apart
miles that can't be counted.
Not together at all.

Greeting the Ocean

August 25, 2024

When I arrived on the Oregon coast
I walked out to greet the ocean.
Something I do every time I'm here.

But this time, I approached the ocean
as a widow.
A word I never considered.
A role I never thought of.
A reality I never wanted.

And so I stood by the Pacific
And I was speechless.

Eventually, I asked her, "Are you alone too?"
"No," she said. "You're here.
And I will catch your tears.
Just as I always have."

I cried
and her waves held me.

Sunsets on the Oregon Coast

Haiku
August 25, 2024

This place of sunsets
colors the memories of
my husband's last breaths.

This Widow Thing

August 28, 2024

I don’t know how to do this widow thing.
Am I expected to wear only black?
Or can I still wear my favorite colors?
Teal, red, purple. Green, yellow, pink.
A part of who I’ve always been.
Do I drape some sort of black net over my face
so my grief is trapped and hidden?
Or am I allowed to show my expression
with all its tracks and tears?
Am I to sing only my husband’s praises, or
if there are complaints, then must I stay silent?
Am I to walk with a shuffle or
can I still stride as if the world is waiting?
As if he is waiting?
As if it’s okay that no one is waiting, and
there is only me?
Am I to only show sadness, solemnity, a
downtrodden mouth, eyes glistening with
tears, instead of eyes that gleam with joy?
Am I supposed to only miss him,
wish to speak to him,
ache with the loss of him,
and never again feel that uplift of heart
that comes from no reason at all but the
shining of the sun? Or the moon?

Am I no longer a wife, with a wedding ring
on my finger?
Am I to take it off, tuck it in a drawer somewhere,
and put on something new? Or keep my finger as
bare as I was on the night I became his wife?
Am I no longer a woman?
Is a widow what I am?
All I am?
All I'll be from now on?
With my husband lost,
is there anything left of me?

Silver

September 2, 2024

The first time I was married,
I was 20 years old. It lasted 17 years.
Ended in divorce.
The second time I was married,
I was 39 years old. It lasted
24 years. 8 months. 19 days.
I chose to leave the first husband.
The second left me, but not by his choice.
He was taken against his will.
And against mine.

I will never be married for 25 years.
I will never have a silver anniversary.
If I was married tomorrow, as soon as the clock
ticks past midnight today,
then I would be 89 years old when
the marriage turned silver.
Not too likely I'll be married tomorrow.
Not too likely I'll be married next week,
next month, next year.

My children will never present me with a silver platter
inscribed *Congratulations on 25 years of marriage!,*
like my first husband and his siblings gave to their parents.
We had a lovely dinner in their honor at a restaurant
nestled on the Lake Michigan shoreline.

I had prime rib. A grasshopper for dessert.
I still remember.
My dinner plate stained red.
My tongue stained green.

On October 9th, 2024, our 25th anniversary,
my husband will have been dead for
3 months and 20 days.
Our marriage will have been dead for
3 months and 20 days.
There will be no platter.
No dinner on the shore of Lake Michigan.
But I think I will place both hands on my
husband's urn and say,
"Happy anniversary, honey,"
anyway.

The Cormorant

September 3, 2024

All day, I watched a cormorant
give up his life on the shore.
He stood for hours, facing the ocean.
Stepped back as waves rolled up to his toes.
I saw him breathe
and stretch his wings
but he never took to flight.
He waited.
Straight. Tall.
I walked out to him and as I drew close,
he tried to run, his legs stiff
and soon useless
and he fell.
I stopped and so did he.
He pulled himself to a stand and looked to the ocean
Again.
I let him be.

From the house, I watched through binoculars.
A jogger going by sent the cormorant into the waves.
He bobbed and rode the current back to shore
where he stood up again.
Straight. Tall.
A dog sent the cormorant out further
and I held my breath as he disappeared under the waves.
But soon, he pulled himself back up on the sand.
He stood.
Straight. Tall.
And then he nested. Rested.
The tide came and washed him away.

I saw his head bob once, twice.
And then he disappeared under the waves.
I cried.

I thought of you, as I watched you for five months.
And two days.
You were hit by a van, run over.
It took time, but you stood up.
Straight. Tall.
You moved through ICU, through a step-down room,
returned to ICU, then stepped down again.
You stood up each time.
Rehab.
You stood up.
You came home, and then fell down
in the middle of the night.
In the hospital, you stood up.
You came home, fell down.
And in the hospital, and then the hospice,
I saw you nest into the bed. Rest.
I was by your side when you washed away
your breath going underwater
and you disappeared.

Get up, I urged the cormorant
until he didn't.
Get up, I urged you
until you didn't.
And now I stand at the edge of the sea.
And I look for you both.

The Movies

September 6, 2024

Remember our delight when our local theater
put in new seats, leather-esque recliners?
We pushed up the shared armrest and turned
the two seats into one big reclining loveseat.
We no longer had to let go of each other as
our arms fell asleep on that invasive armrest.
Our fingers entwined.
Without an armrest, in the new seats,
your hand always found its way to my thigh
after you ate your fill of popcorn.
I never pushed you away, though I did complain
about the leftover butter stains on my pants.
I could rest my head on your shoulder.
You played movie reviewer into my ear.
And my pants smelled like butter and popcorn
even after I washed them.

I've been to the movies without you now.
The day after you died, the kids took me
to see *Inside Out 2,*
a title that so matched how I was feeling.
I ate popcorn. I laughed at the screen.
Cried too. The dark theater gave me permission.
Though the tears had nothing to do
with what was happening on the screen.
I left the armrest down.
There was no need to push it up.
Your seat was empty.
My arm didn't fall asleep without yours
cutting off my circulation.

My bloodflow.
My heartbeat.
But these were cut off anyway
by the weight of your absence.
I wiped my own fingers on my pants
so I could smell the butter
and think of you.

Lazarus Has Nothing to Do with It

Prose Poem
Written back home in Waukesha, Wisconsin
September 24, 2024

Grief support group. A video. People on the screen talk so we don't have to. Crying. Loneliness. Hopelessness. A man talks about how he preferred Solitude, before his wife died. Now, he says, he is not Solitary. He is "Utterly Alone." Then a woman, folded over her own knees, sits in a bathtub. She's fully dressed. There is no water. And somehow, we are to believe she is thinking of Killing Herself. Thinking so we don't have to. I nod. I know that Posture. Then the screen is split with a Bereaved man's wide, wide, wide smile. He rhapsodizes,

"Jesus wept! Jesus wept!"

The book of John. Chapter 11. *Jesus wept. Then said the Jews, Behold how he loved him! And some of them said, Could not this man, who opened the eyes of the blind, have kept Lazarus from dying? Jesus groaned. The grave was a cave, and a stone lay upon it. Jesus said, Take away the stone. They said, Lord, he has been dead four days. Jesus said, Did I not tell you, if you believe, you will see the glory of God? Then they took away the stone. And Jesus lifted up his eyes, and said, Father, I am grateful that you have heard me. And then he cried with a loud voice, Lazarus, come forth. And Lazarus came forth, bound hand and foot with graveclothes, and his face was bound about with a napkin. Jesus said to them, Loose him, and let him go.*

Let him go.

Jesus wept. The shortest verse in the bible. Shortest Grief too. Jesus snapped his fingers and brought Lazarus back to Life. Jesus was grateful that God listened.

And this Bereaved man rhapsodizes on screen, and praises Jesus for experiencing Grief, experiencing, he says, what we Feel. Sharing, he says, what we Feel. I think, What? My Grief has lasted longer than two minutes. And my husband has not been returned to Life. He has not been loosed. He has not been let go. When I say this to the group, they rhapsodize, with wide, wide, wide smiles, "But the resurrection! The resurrection!" But Jesus didn't resurrect Lazarus. He didn't send Lazarus to Heaven, where he would supposedly be in

a Better Place.

Or so I'm told.

Jesus brought Lazarus back here. To Earth. To his Family. To his Friend. Jesus. To Life.

To Life.

When I leave the grief support group this day, I know I will not be back. Even if he is in Heaven, my husband would want to be Home. His Better Place. Ours. And no matter how many times I snap my fingers and look, look, look hard, for the glory of God, I am not heard.

I am still Utterly Alone.

And I am not grateful.

Listening

Haiku
September 24, 2024

Ear pressed to his urn,
I reach for my husband's voice.
Nothing. Just silence.

Silver Anniversary

Written 6 days after the anniversary
October 15, 2024

On our silver anniversary
the only silver I see is
my memory of your hair.
It was black and curly on
the day we married.
I loved to twine and lock
my fingers in your curls
and pull you hard to me
while lovemaking
guiding your mouth wherever
I wanted it.
And I wanted it.
That was years ago.
When I was taking care of you
I brushed your silver as gently
as I brushed our baby girl's.
And the last of you I touched
before I left your body behind
before it was burned to silver ash
was your hair.
On our silver anniversary
I wished I'd touched you more.
I wish to touch you again.

I Wish I Couldn’t Read

On the day I received a 7-page single-spaced report from a police investigator, detailing the accident second by second
October 23, 2024

Security camera video begins.
At 6:00 p.m., Giorgio is observed standing
on the sidewalk on the northwest corner.
He is wearing a black long-sleeve shirt, tan khaki pants,
carrying an orange and black shoulder bag.
I observe my cell phone, noting the time, and think that
my husband is done with work and heading home.
To me.
At seventeen seconds, Giorgio is still standing.
On my computer screen, my client’s face appears.
He smiles.
I smile back.
At twenty-three seconds, Giorgio enters the marked crosswalk
to travel southbound, crossing West State Street.
My client and I talk about his novel about a soundless boy
who takes care of dogs who are killed in a lab during World War II.
The boy wonders silently if he is a murderer.
At twenty-four seconds, a small black SUV makes a left turn.
Giorgio pauses and the vehicle does not yield,
but continues past him.
At twenty-nine seconds, a white 4-door SUV makes a left turn.
Giorgio pauses. The vehicle does not yield,
but continues past him.
My client and I examine his sentences, his words, where he
paragraphs, where he uses an ellipsis, a dash, a period.
Our voices rise and fall, pause and pass.

At thirty seconds, Giorgio stops walking.
At thirty-two seconds, a silver minivan makes a left turn.
It does not yield,
but continues past him.
Giorgio looks over his shoulder, back at the sidewalk.
In my client's novel, numbers are important.
Measurements. Lengths. Widths. Weight.
Time.
At thirty-seven seconds, Giorgio continues to walk in the crosswalk.
At thirty-nine seconds, a blue passenger van turns left
and enters the crosswalk.
It does not yield. It does not pass.
Giorgio turns and puts his hands approximately hood-height onto the van.
At forty seconds, the van collides with Giorgio.
Words are important too, I say.
One word and the whole meaning changes.
Collides.

Did you scream? Did you see the driver, his eyes wide, blank,
not registering that there is a man in front of him?
A man on the hood of his van? In his windshield?
Breaking his windshield.
A man. A father. A grandfather.
My husband.

One word and the whole meaning changes.
The video is soundless.

Giorgio is carried on the hood of the van for approximately two seconds
before falling off.
At forty-three seconds, the van runs over Giorgio.
The van runs over Giorgio.
Over.
One word and the whole meaning changes.
Numbers are important too.
The van weighs 4464 pounds.
Four-thousand, four-hundred, and sixty-four pounds.
At forty-five seconds, Giorgio is laying in the street.

When did you stop breathing? When did your heart stop?
Did you see the sky? Or did you see Heaven?
Did you hear the sirens and know they were
for you?
Did you feel a stranger begin CPR?
Did you feel your heart start again? Your eyes open?

At one minute and fifteen seconds, a maroon SUV pulls across lanes. Flashers on. It blocks traffic.
Security camera video ends.

Did you feel the paramedics cutting off your clothes?
Your favorite shirt? Black, long sleeves.
The shirt I gave you for Christmas.

At 6:42 p.m., Giorgio is admitted to the hospital with life-threatening status due to head trauma.
The police follow.
At 6:45 p.m., I see my cell phone screen light up with a call.
I do not recognize the number, and so I let it go to voicemail.
Numbers are important.
I finish with my client.

On the stretcher in the ER, Giorgio screams for help.
He thrashes and is restrained.
The police say he is combative. Uncooperative.
They leave without asking for a statement.
Giorgio has brain trauma. Brain bleed. His body is out of control.
Words are important.
One word and the whole meaning changes.
Giorgio is combative.
Giorgio is combatting death.
At 6:55, I call my voicemail.
The recording tells me my husband is in the ER at a hospital.
Please call.
The voice gives a number.
Numbers are important. Time.
Ten minutes after the recording, I call the number I don't recognize.
"Your husband was struck by a vehicle. You need to come in. Hurry."
Hurry.
One word and the whole meaning changes.

I hear you screaming for help before I see you. I call your name.
I touch your arm. "It's me, it's me," I say. "I'm here."
You scream for help. Your eyes are wide, blank.
You don't see me.
I faint.
One skull fracture.
Two skull fractures.
Multiple skull fractures.
Numbers are important. Even when there are too many
to count.
Fracture of the T-10 vertebrae in spine.
Fracture of the left tibia.
Possible neck fracture.
Fracture of ribs 8 and 9.
Multiple brain bleeds.
Brain swelling.
Severe traumatic brain injury.
Severe. Multiple. Severe. Multiple.
Traumatic.
One word and the whole meaning changes.
I sit by your side. I hold your hand.
ICU. Step-down room. ICU. Step-down room.
NG tube. Neck brace. Back brace.
Feeding tube. IV. IV. IV. Catheter.
Rehab. Wheelchair. Walker.
Home. Home health aides. Nurse. Occupational therapist.
Physical therapist. Speech therapist. Neurologist. Urologist.
Orthopedist. Otolaryngologist. Ophthalmologist.
UTI. Stomach ulceration. Vomiting blood.
Giorgio stops eating.

Ambulance.
Hospital.
Hospice.
On June 19th, I watch you let go of your last breath.
I sit by your side. I hold your hand.
My eyes are wide and blank.
I am soundless.
The driver is given a citation for failure to yield to a pedestrian.
He pays $73.
Seventy-three dollars.
Numbers are important.
Does he wonder if he is a murderer?
Silently?
One word and the whole meaning changes.

On October 21st, I receive a 7-page letter from a police investigator.
There are videos. I don't watch them.
But with these words, on these 7 pages, I see you.
I see you raise your hands to the hood of the van.
Both hands. You face the van. You face the man.
You are combative.
Help.
Words are important.
One word and the whole meaning changes.
Numbers are important too.
Seventy-three dollars.
I wish I couldn't read.
I am soundless.

Nightclothes

November 22, 2024

I always wore pajamas
with my first husband.
From our first overnights in college
to the 17th year of our marriage.
Pajamas from 18 years old
to 38 years old.
Mostly nightshirts.
Always underwear.
To make sure I had a moment
of warning.
With my second husband,
I slept in a nightshirt on
our first overnight.
But then . . . it disappeared.
And I never bought another.
For the 25 years of our marriage
I slept in the nude, and so did he.
But I was dressed in his skin
in his arms
his breath warm on my neck.
Safe.

Now that he’s gone
without warning
not by his choice
I still sleep in the nude
with his memory.
But covered up to my nose in
a sheet
and two blankets
and an orange cat curved behind my knees.

Last Scrap

November 25, 2024

Today, I brought your last bit of clothing
to Goodwill.
Two winter jackets, one leather.
Two fall hoodies.
One denim button-up jacket.
I gave you the denim late last fall
not knowing you'd never have a chance
to wear it.
I found it at Goodwill.
Today, it went back.
As I removed each jacket from its hook,
I pulled it on.
Wrapped you over my shoulders
zipped up the front.
Except for the denim one. It was never filled
with you.
It was filled with lost wishes. Lost wants.
Lost love.

I thought about keeping one, to wrap around me
on cold days. Lonely nights.
But all the sleeves went well past my fingertips.
They hung on me, lifeless.
And I didn't need the reminder.
So I'm letting them keep someone else warm
instead.
You would like that.

Closet

December 20, 2024

Two weeks after your death,
I give all your shirts to Goodwill.
Some, you haven't worn in years.
Others still have the price tags.
All are stuffed so tightly on the rod,
it is difficult to free them.
You always had trouble getting rid of things.
Including me.

I give away your pants, shorts, suits,
swim trunks, ties, belts.
I throw away your underwear and socks.
The clothing closet and the dresser drawers
are empty.
So I turn and face what I call your "hoarder's closet"
as a joke.
But it isn't a joke.
It's a secret.
Even from me.
You told me to stay out.

Inside, the framework that held the shelves
has broken from the weight.
The shelves collapsed and rested
on the piles of things on the shelf below
and below and below.

I have to move and remove very carefully
starting from the top
or else the closet interior will fall
like an avalanche
of unknowns.
I worry I could drown
be buried alive
in detritus.
Years and years of detritus.
Of secrets.

Oh, the things I pull out.

Old CDs and DVDs and VHSs and cassettes.
Empty jewel cases. Most cracked beyond use.
Books. Unread. Receipts still inside.
Newspapers. TV Guides.
Yearbooks and autograph books
that belonged to strangers.
Bought at antique stores.
Christmas ornaments that never hung on our tree.
Sports figures. Action figures. Cartoon figures.
Many miniature rubber duckies, all made up to look
like anything but a duck.
Change.
Photos.

Notebooks.
Letters.

As I unload shelf after shelf
fill bag after bag,
place in piles marked
Goodwill
Garbage
Keep,
I brush at my sleeves, over and over.
I want to take a shower.
So much dust. So much dirt.
So much I didn't know.

The Keep pile is the smallest.

In the second to last collapsed shelf,
I find a piece of cardboard.
On one side, in black marker,
your name. An arrow pointing up.
On the other, my name.
With a question mark.
It's from the first time we met, in an airport,
face to face
after getting to know each other on the internet.

I remember laughing.
I remember the way your arms felt around me
that first time.
Nothing between us.

Now, I hold the cardboard sign with our names
and then carefully place it in the Keep pile.

After I hire a handyman to build a new framework,
lay new shelves
I put the sign back in the closet. On the top shelf.
And everything else I put in the closet,
I choose to be there.
No secrets.
There was so much I didn't know.
But at least I know this.
You kept the sign that marked our meeting.
And you loved me.

One Year Later

January 17, 2025

I am watching the clock.
It is almost 6:04 p.m.
on January 17, 2025.
One year ago, on this day,
at this time,
you were crossing the intersection at
6th and State in downtown Milwaukee.
An intersection I've never seen, but
will never forget.
You walked with the light.
You were within the crosswalk.
And a man named Kevin
a man I've never seen, but
will never forget
White
Retired
Widowed
76 years old
drove his passenger van right into you.
You saw him coming.
Held your hands out in supplication.
But it didn't stop him.
He said he was on his way to church.

My phone rang around 6:45.
I was busy and ignored it.
Busy.
Always busy.

I didn't know until 6:55
that our whole world changed
at 6:04 p.m., January 17, 2024.

And it would keep on changing
until your life ended on June 19.
After that, my world would
never be the same.

A year
since the accident
Seven months
since you died
I am still angry.
Still mired in a grief so dark,
I just can't see through it.

And a man named Kevin
is still driving.
He is out $73
the fee for a citation
Failure To Yield To A Pedestrian.
His life goes on
as if January 17, 2024,
never happened.

Your life doesn't go on.
Mine is frozen.

It is exactly 6:04 p.m. now
exactly one year later.
I wonder if Kevin is
on his way to church.

I pray for anyone who gets in
his Holy way.
Closing my eyes, I think of you.
I can no longer do anything more.

My Language

February 7, 2025

I was a part of “we”, but now I’m “I”.
A part of “us”, but now I’m “me”.
Part of “our”, but now I’m “my”.

His death is changing my language.

When I speak to him, only I hear.
There are no interruptions or replies.
My “—” and “!,?” has turned into “. . .”

I no longer refer to him in the present tense
“is” has faded to “was”
“are” to “were”.

His life is now my third person past tense.
But my grief is still very much
in first person.

His death is changing my language.

Your Image

February 13, 2025

Over and over, I see that final image of you
sent to me by the investigator who attempted
to put your accident into words.
I see you with my eyes closed.
I see you with my eyes wide open.
And I don't want to see you
at all.

You turned to face the passenger van
a 2007 Toyota Sienna
blue
as it bore down on you as you walked
Within the crosswalk
With the light
Within your rights
The van weighed 4464 pounds.
You turned and faced it
held out both your hands
In supplication
In desperation
In the most intense act of bravery I've ever seen
though I didn't see it. I pictured it. From his words.
You placed your hands on the hood of the van
and then it hit you anyway.
I was 18.7 miles away.
At home.

I don't want this to be the image that stays with me
of you.

I want to see you with your arms open, for me.
Or your arms wrapped around our daughter.
I want to see you in your recliner
Your laptop in your lap
Your phone in your hand
As you write
Play a word scramble game
And watch television
All at the same time.
But still turn to look at me
and smile.

I want to open my eyes in the middle of the night
and see the shadow of you next to me
Your head, shoulders, waist, hips
creating an intimate mountain range
and I recognize every inch.

I want to see you laughing.

But instead, over and over, I see you
Your hands out
Trying to do the impossible.
Trying to stop what you didn't start.
Trying to keep our marriage intact and
not broken in pieces by the impact
of a 4464-pound vehicle
and a man who wasn't paying any attention
while he was on his way to church (he said).

As if being devout would make this right.
As if praying could make this right.
Even God won’t make this right.

I will keep trying to see you.
I will close and open my eyes
until the image of you with your arms open
to me
is the only thing I see.

The Missing Hour

February 13, 2025

I miss him the most at night
when the house is quiet and dark
except for the bedside lamps on either side
of our bed.

I miss the rhythm as he brushed his teeth
His tuneless hum as he finished
His lumbering like a bear to a nearby wall
and scratching his back against the corner.
His growl of pleasure like a bear's as well.

I miss the sink of the mattress as he curled into bed
Draped an arm around my waist
Rested his hand upon my breast
My body a set of grooves worn by his fit.
We were more than a puzzle.
There was no searching and sorting.
Only two pieces.
Joined.

I miss his murmur of goodnight
which often drifted into a joke
My laughter, then his, shaking the bed
in a different way than it used to shake
when his hand on my breast was a signal
for something other than rest and ease and comfort.

It took years to create this comfort.
So layered, so prevalent, that I feel it even now
when he's gone.

At night, when I miss him the most,
I brush my teeth on my own.
Pat the wall where he used to scratch.
Turn off both bedside lights, but
only turn down my side of the bed.

I lay on my side
rest my own hand on my breast
and think of him.
My tears shake the bed now.

Compensation

February 28, 2025

I am being offered "compensation"
For my husband.
For his life,
His breath,
His soul,
His love.
For our life together, spanning
a few months shy of twenty-five years
of marriage
But knowing each other far longer.
The compensation comes in dollars
Not in hours of company
Hands being held
Kisses on the neck
Good mornings, good nights,
Laughter
Tears
Arguments
Making up
I still call his name out loud
when I have something to tell him.
Am I to curl up in bed with money?
Cry on the shoulder of a dollar bill.
Place twenties on his recliner
to watch favorite tv shows together.

Will the dollar sign know what I'm
going to say before I say it?
Will it call me by the name that only he
called me?
"Compensation."
As if any dollar amount could bring back
what I've lost.
Blood money.

Absent

May 16, 2025

For eleven months, you have been gone.
For three months, I have been silent.
I spoke for eight months
and it made no difference.
But after three months of my silence
nothing has changed.
I am still alone.

I have not been silent inside.
Inside, I have been screaming
and crying
raging
and pleading.
Outside, I open my eyes in the morning
move through my day
close my eyes at night.
But I hear the chaos within.
It comes out in dreams.

Dreams of running away.
Or chasing others.
Dreams of your voice coming from
a different face.
Seeing someone else I recognize,
but still know it's you.
Dreams that are impossible.
And when I wake,
I face that impossibility.

One morning, I open my eyes before my alarm.
When I look over at your side of the bed,
I see a hole in the wall, just beyond.
A man sits there, a bald man, heavy,
reading a newspaper.
He looks at me and smiles.
Waves.
I wave back and return to sleep.
When I wake later, the hole is gone.
But I know it held your father
who died before I met you.

I feel he was telling me you're all right.
And he was telling me that I'm not.
That day, I decide
to stay in bed.
I get up today.

I think about these poems
and about how I've gone silent.
My writing voice never silent before
but beginning to move away from silence
to missing.
Disappearing.
Dying.
Like you.

And I just can't take another loss.

So today, I sit down to write again.
My voice is slow
and pain-filled.
But I think of your father
and I smile.

Phantom Limb

May 16, 2025

I'm told that in grief, the brain keeps looking
for the person who is missing.
Just like a phantom limb.
I think of all the ways I look for you.

When someone steps out of the bus depot to walk
toward home.
When our dog suddenly sits up and looks at
your chair.
Last thing at night when I look at your side of
the bed
And first thing in the morning when I look at it.
Again.
When I hear your laugh. Your sigh. Your groan
of discontent.

You are my phantom limb, a part of me I've lost
but still feel is here, somewhere. Still connected
to me.
A part of my brain just does not accept that
you're gone.
Or maybe it's a part of
my heart.

The Birth of a Widow

June 2, 2025

It was when I saw her outside the MetroMarket
that I realized it.
She was a hibiscus tree, about five feet tall
almost as tall as I am
and she was all alone on a pallet.

There were other hibiscus trees, standing together
in pairs, in groups, twos and threes, even four,
like couples, or couples with young children.
But this hibiscus, almost as tall as I am
stood all by herself. Separate.

It's been almost a year since my husband died.
Eleven months and a few weeks.

I was at the store to pick up cook-out food
to enjoy Memorial Day with my grown children.
Our child, and my children from my first marriage.
Memorial Day.
A day of remembrance.

I remembered. Even though he didn't die in a war.
He was struck and run over by a passenger van.
He was killed.

I walked to the single hibiscus tree and I stood
with my back to all the others.
I said one word.

"Hi."
Then I picked her up and took her inside
and set her in a grocery cart.
We shopped for the cook-out food together.

Seeing her there, alone. Separate.
Away from the other hibiscus who gathered
in couples and families
I saw myself.

I realized then, fully, not just as the word, but
down to my bones. To my cells. In my heart.
I am a widow.
No longer a wife.
A lover.
A partner.
Not even a best friend.

Neither was she.

I took her home
for the company.

Not So Free as Free

June 8, 2025

When I was born, I belonged to my parents.
They told me I was theirs
until they gave me away to the man that they wanted
to call son.

In that marriage, I belonged to my husband.
He told me I was his.
He was the owner, and I was the property.
I didn't know any other way to be.

But I dreamed anyway.

I met my last husband while still married to the first.
He held my hand, not with the clench of ownership
but the tenderness of side-by-side.
With his hand in mine, I broke the shackles.

Neither of us owned the other,
But we belonged together.
Our hands joined
for twenty-five years.

And then he died.

Now, I am, for the first time, only my own.
No one holds my hand
or shackles my wrist.
There is no one to give me away.

I am the freedom of one
but I miss the freedom
of two.

My New Vocabulary Words

List Poem
June 9, 2025

Neuro ICU (Neurological Intensive Care Unit)
Skull Fracture
Two Skull Fractures.
Three.
Multiple Skull Fractures.
Brain Bleed.
Brain Swelling.
TBI (Traumatic Brain Injury)
T-10 Vertebrae Fracture
Left Tibia Fracture
Ribs #7 and #8 Fracture
Possible Neck Fracture
Neck Cuff
Nasal Cannula
MRI (Magnetic Resonance Imaging)
CT scan (Computed Tomography Scan)
Feeding Tube
Urinary Catheter
Step-down room
PA (Physician's Assistant)
APA (Assistant Physician's Assistant)
Hospitalist (changes every 48 hours)
TPN (Total Parenteral Nutrition)
PICC line (Peripherally Inserted Central Catheter)
Rehab

Rehab Release
PT (Physical Therapist)
OT (Occupational Therapist)
Speech Therapist (Why not ST?)
At-Home Nurse (AHN?)
UTI (Urinary Tract Infection)
Ulceration
Palliative care
Hospice
Valium
Morphine
Keep him comfortable.
Goodbye.
Passed.
Dead.
Gone.

Limbo

June 17, 2025

I watch the sun set over the Pacific Ocean
and wonder how anyone could watch this
the sky   sea   red orange purple   pelicans   glory
and not believe in God

and then I remember how you looked in the ER
and wonder how anyone could see you
the blood broken bones purple black blue chaos
and believe in God.

I've seen both, and I have no idea where I stand
except with one foot in belief and the other in disbelief
my arms spread wide with anger. Raised fists.
Tears.

When I do believe in God while watching the ocean,
I admire, but don't like him very much.
And when I don't believe, when I remember and remember,
I seethe and still don't like him.

I guess that makes me an atheist
or an agnostic
or a blasphemer.
But I know it makes me a widow.

The Night Before the Last Morning

One year ago, I didn’t know
it was the last time I would say goodnight,
Smooth your hair, kiss your forehead
because your lips were nonresponsive.

Hospice meant you were going to die
but it’s amazing how my mind
could convince me differently.
I didn’t say goodbye.

Just Goodnight. See you tomorrow.

I left you sleeping, or doing whatever it was
you were doing as your body prepared to let go.
I wonder often if your nonresponsive lips tried
to call to me. *Wait. These are our last moments.*

At home, I probably watched some television.
Talked to the dog. Talked to the cat.
Then I tucked myself in to my side of the bed.
The bed that was still ours. Then.

I fell asleep quickly, and I do know that
my sleep was the sleep of the dead
or the sleep of the one being left behind.
I wish now that I had dreamed. Of you.

The phone call would come early in the morning.
But I didn't know that yet.
I didn't know that I only had a few hours left
to be a wife.

Goodnight.

The First Day After the First Anniversary of Your Death

June 20, 2025

When midnight struck on your death anniversary,
I breathed a sigh of relief.
It was over, this first year.
It was done.

But when I woke on this morning,
the first day after the first year,
You were still gone
and I still wore grief like a cloak.

It wraps around my throat sometimes.
And sometimes, it drapes my shoulders.
If it falls off, I catch it tight,
throttle it with both fists.

I drag it behind me
or I wear it upon me
and I wonder when my fingers will open,
all on their own, and let it go.

Leaving only you and me
who you were
and who I am
now that you're gone.

The Cliché

Essay

My husband died by cliché.

You know how, whenever someone is going to take a risk and argues against it possibly being deadly, he or she says, "You could die tomorrow by stepping off a curb and getting run over by a bus!"? That's essentially what my husband did, except in his case, it was a 4600-pound passenger van.

On January 17, 2024, my husband Michael left his job at MATC (Milwaukee Area Technical College) and crossed the intersection of 6th and State in downtown Milwaukee. Michael was a fastidious pedestrian, largely because he was terrified of cars. After taking driver's ed in high school, he bought a used car, drove it home and parked it—never to take his driver's test and never to drive again. On this day, Michael carefully waited for, then stepped into the street with the permission of the shining Walk signal. He stayed well within the crosswalk. A 76-year-old man, turning left, hit Michael, sending him up on the hood of the van, into the windshield, then dropping him to the ground. The man then ran over Michael with all four tires.

Michael suffered a severe traumatic brain injury, multiple skull fractures, a fracture of the T-10 vertebrae in his back, a possible neck fracture, a fracture of the left tibia and two of his left ribs. He lost the hearing in his left ear and most of the vision in his left eye. Before the paramedics came, he was not breathing and he had no pulse. A witness started CPR and Michael revived and was transported to the hospital with life-threatening injuries. He struggled hard to recover for five months, spending six weeks in the hospital, cycling between Neurological ICU and a step-down room, three weeks in rehab, then coming home for just over a month before he returned to the hospital and ultimately, hospice.

His body was invaded with an NG tube, a feeding tube, a catheter, PICC lines, and too many IVs to count. He was stuffed into the MRI machine multiple times. He suffered infections and respiratory illnesses, and a UTI. Ultimately, the traumatic brain injury could not be overcome, and my lovely husband, who faithfully stepped off a curb with the full belief he would reach the other side, died on June 19th, 2024.

He was fifty-nine years old. We were four months shy of our twenty-fifth wedding anniversary.

I've spent much of the nine months since his death gazing blankly straight ahead, and muttering, "What the hell?" If you'll excuse another cliché, while Michael was hit by a 4600-pound passenger van, I feel like I've been hit by a Mack truck. Depending on the type of Mack truck, that's somewhere between 23,000 and 92,000 pounds.

It's parked right on top of me. I crawl and carry it on my back every day, like a monstrous turtle shell.

Michael was a writer, and so am I, with a total of 19 books between the two of us. We both teach (taught) writers. Our horror of the cliché goes deep. And now . . . a cliché killed my husband. And another cliché holds me captive.

I wish I could write a manual, a how-to on grief. But I just don't think that's possible, because much of grief is unspeakable and unbearable and, unfortunately, unavoidable. While Michael was still alive and going through the five months between the accident and his death, I didn't even realize I was in grief. I focused so hard on being positive, for him, for our daughter, for my kids from my first marriage, for our granddaughter. Even for our dog and cats. If I stayed positive, I thought, he will survive.

"You will make it," I said to him, and he listened. "You will return to work by the end of summer." I lived in a dark void, with light shining all around it, which is what I focused on. Ignore the dark, get to the light.

I had moments that I didn't recognize as grief. I'd burst into tears over an item that was sold out in a grocery store, or traffic that was just moving too slow.

I became enraged when I stopped on the way home from the hospital one night to buy a strawberry shake at Culver's, and the lid wasn't properly fastened. I picked it up from my cupholder to bring it inside, and it fell, splattering pink ice cream all over the inside of my car. I grabbed the cup, threw it into the parking lot, and stomped on it, getting pink ice cream all over myself too, and I screamed.

But then I shook it off. Literally and metaphorically. Go toward the light, I thought. Stay positive. He will return to work by the end of the summer.

Michael's memory, seriously affected at first, seemed to be coming back. He began to walk with a walker. First, the feeding tube was removed, then the catheter. He began to eat, graduating from liquid to pureed to soft to normal. We both cheered the day he ate a peanut butter and jelly sandwich, his favorite. One day, he managed to slowly climb the stairs to the third floor of our condo and then move with his walker onto our deck. He sat in the sun for the first time in months, he looked at all of the flowers I'd planted during the spring he missed, he took deep breaths of city-fresh air, and he said, "I'm going to make it."

Then, he developed a UTI and an infection in his stomach where the feeding tube used to be. He went back into the hospital, deteriorated, and then died after only a few days in hospice.

The dark void for me became very, very black. There was no light.

During that final hospital stay, I thought he'd given up. He seemed to be refusing to eat. The nurses were frustrated, the doctors had no answers. "Why aren't you eating?" I asked him.

"I am," he insisted. "I eat everything."

But the nurses showed me his trays. Nothing was touched. The doctors told me to forget all about a healthy diet and just bring him everything he found irresistible. I brought in chicken nuggets from McDonalds, a Choco Brownie Extreme Blizzard from Dairy Queen, chicken dumpling soup and meatloaf from Spring City, our favorite restaurant.

He ate none of it.

I pleaded, I ranted, I raved. I don't know how many times I walked out on him in frustration. "You can't give up!" I said. "Your daughter needs you. I need you. Come on!" He'd look at me helplessly and I'd run from the room.

Once, I said the unthinkable.

If I could erase time, if I could take every word back, I would. I was just so angry. After another uneaten meal, I stood at the door to his room, ready to walk out again. I turned back to him and hissed, "I wish I'd never married you."

I have no doubt he heard.

When I tried McDonalds again, I sat next to him, with him in his hospital bed, and me in a chair. We shared the tray. "I'm going to eat with you," I said. I watched as he picked up a French fry. He held it for twenty minutes. Then he put it down. He hadn't taken a single bite.

"Michael," I said. "Aren't you going to eat that?"

He looked bewildered again. "What are you talking about?" he said. "I ate it all."

I pointed at his tray, at the six untouched nuggets, the full envelope of fries, the one rejected fry that was placed by itself.

He looked and said, "See? It's all gone."

It was then that I realized how derailed his brain had become. And I also realized how awful I'd been, to a man who just didn't understand. Who was trying to survive, but his brain was telling him otherwise.

A few days later, Michael was spending most of his time sleeping. After talking with the doctors, who told me that the ending was inevitable, I agreed to pull all nutritional support and to move Michael to hospice.

He slept; I went on autopilot.

Michael was moved by ambulance to the hospice. I followed as fast as I could to this place that I'd never seen. A representative came to speak to me at the hospital, and she showed me photos. It looked lovely. I tried to tell myself that it looked hopeful, and that there was still a chance he would suddenly find the cognizance to recover.

But I wasn't prepared for what I saw when I walked into his room that first time. For the last several weeks, he'd been in that hospital bed, twisting and turning, sometimes even sleeping with his head at the foot. The sheets were mostly twisted around his body, or scattered on the floor. A special blanket that I'd brought from home disappeared.

But in that hospice room, it was quiet. He was in a bed with clean, white smooth sheets, and he was covered with a soft blue blanket. His head rested on a pillow. There were huge windows, and French doors that opened to a patio overlooking a small lake.

And Michel slept. Peacefully. He looked like himself.

He arrived on Friday evening. Early in the morning on Wednesday, our daughter and I were by his side as he quietly slipped away.

A few minutes later, my daughter stepped outside for a moment of solitude and deep breathing. I leaned over Michael, pressed my lips to his left ear, and hoped he was now able to hear my voice. "I love you," I said. "You were never a cliché to me."

And now?

The black void is still here, and I am trying to work my way through it. Without him. The black void that is caused by his absence. Days are hard; nights are harder. I do the things I need to do. I teach. I write. Offer comfort to our daughter, to my three kids from my first marriage, to my granddaughter, to my dog, to my cats. I do my best to offer comfort to myself as well, but I've found that difficult. I keep hearing myself, saying, "I wish I'd never married you," and seeing his bewildered look.

I know now that when I said that, I wasn't really saying that I wished I'd never married him. Never spent the four months shy of twenty-five years together. I was saying, "I wish I'd never married you, so that you couldn't leave me now."

But I hear my words, and I damn myself over and over again.

When the void is at its darkest, I close my eyes and I see him again in hospice. At peace. Sleeping. The sheets undisturbed, the blanket warm and smooth. His peacefulness let me know that I'd made the right decision. And that the decision was made out of the deepest kind of love.

I hope, somewhere in his damaged brain, more damaged than the doctors and nurses knew, than the specialists and therapists knew, than even I knew, he heard me tell him I love him. And that, in the way of husbands and wives who have been together for decades, he heard the truth behind my words when I said, "I wish I'd never married you."

I just didn't want him to leave. Me.

When I said those words, I was preparing to experience another cliché: tis better to have loved and lost than never to have loved at all. I was working hard to believe it. I still am. The loss is harder than anything I've ever experienced. But the love is the best.

Michael lived the cliché when he stepped off that curb. And now, I'm the one living a cliché: you don't know what you've got till it's gone.

About Kathie Giorgio

Kathie Giorgio is the critically acclaimed author of eight novels, two story collections, one essay collection, and five poetry books, including *Let Me Tell You, Let Me Sing!* (Kelsay Books, 2025). A Pushcart nominee in fiction and poetry, she's been awarded the Outstanding Achievement Award from the WI Library Association, the Silver Pen Award for Literary Excellence, the Pencraft Award for Literary Excellence, and the Eric Hoffer Award in Fiction.

Her poetry won runner-up in the 2021 Rosebud Magazine Poetry Prize, first prize in the Wisconsin Writers Association's Jade Ring contest, and was included in the Poetry Leaves exhibition in Waterford, MI. Kathie is a two-time winner of the Zona Gale Short Fiction Award, and her work was performed on stage for the Stories on Stage series at Su Teatro Theatre in Boulder, CO. She's included in lists of the top 21 Wisconsin writers of the 21st century.

Besides being a writer, Giorgio is Director and Founder of the international creative writing studio, AllWriters' Workplace & Workshop LLC. AllWriters' offers online and on-site courses and workshops in all genres and abilities of creative writing, as well as coaching and editing services. Thousands of writers worldwide have gotten their start at AllWriters', and thousands have continued their career there. Giorgio has taught for 31 years.

Kathie lives in Waukesha, WI. Three of her adult children, Christopher, Andy, and Olivia, live close by, along with her granddaughter, Maya Mae. One adult child, Katie, has wandered off to Louisiana where she teaches math at the University of Louisiana–Lafayette and lives among the mathematicians and alligators.

kathiegiorgio.org
www.allwritersworkshop.com

www.ingramcontent.com/pod-product-compliance
Lightning Source LLC
LaVergne TN
LVHW090535110826
845146LV00003B/1105

* 9 7 9 8 9 0 1 4 6 7 1 9 0 *